123s Colors & ABCs

Contents

ABCs of the Bible 2
123s of the Bible 18
Colors of the Bible 34

Warner Press Kids
educate • nurture • inspire
www.warnerpress.org

© 2011 Warner Press, Inc
All rights reserved   Made in the USA
30580029316

ABCs of the Bible

A is for **ark**. Noah built an ark for two animals of every kind.

B is for **boat**. Baby Moses was placed in a basket-boat.

Two different kinds of boats. Both were used to help God's people.

Genesis 6; Exodus 2:1-10

C is for **cross**. Jesus died on a cross to save us from our sins.

He rose again three days later.

John 3:16

D is for **desert**. John the Baptist lived in the desert.

E is for **eat**. John the Baptist ate locusts and wild honey.

Mark 1:1-9

F is for **fish**. Peter and Andrew were fishermen.

G is for **Galilee**. They fished on a lake in Galilee.

Luke 5:1-11

H is for **harp**. David, the shepherd boy, played a harp.

I is for **instruments**. We can make music with instruments to praise the Lord.

1 Samuel 16:16-23; Psalm 150

J is for **Jesus**. Jesus loves you.
Jesus loves all His children.

Matthew 19:14

K is for **king**. Jacob's children were a nation of kings.

L is for **ladder**. Jacob once had a dream that angels were climbing a ladder to heaven.

Genesis 28:11-22

M is for **mountains**.

Jesus teaches us that if we have faith, we can move mountains!

Matthew 17:20

N is for **nature**. All of nature was created by God's hand and voice.

Genesis 1

O is for **offering**. **P** is for **prayer**. Whenever we pray,
we offer our thanks to Jesus for His blessings.
We also offer Jesus our lives so that we can live for Him.

Psalm 116:17

Q is for the **Queen** of Sheba. **R** is for **rock**. The Queen of Sheba stood by King Solomon. King Solomon was wise. He believed that God's words were like a rock that you could firmly stand on.

1 Kings 10:1-13

S is for **stone**. **T** is for the **Ten Commandments**.

God wrote the Ten Commandments on a stone.

God gave the stones to Moses to teach God's children.

Exodus 20

U is for **unselfish**. **V** is for **vanished**.

Our unselfish Lord vanished into the clouds at His ascension.

Mark 16:1-20

W is for **wise**. **X** is for **Xerxes**. King Xerxes gave a crown and robes to Mordecai, honoring this wise man who saved the king's life.

Esther 6:1-3; 7:15

Y is for **yes**. **Z** is for **Zacchaeus**. Jesus told Zacchaeus to come down out of the tree. Zacchaeus said "yes" when he obeyed the Lord.

Luke 19:5-6

123s of the Bible

God has **1 (ONE)** Son. His name is Jesus.

Luke 2

God sent **2 (TWO)** of every kind of animal to Noah's ark.

Genesis 6:17-20

The king put **3 (THREE)** men in the furnace because they loved God.

Daniel 3

A man was very sick and could not walk.
His **4 (FOUR)** friends carried him to Jesus to be healed.

Mark 2:1-12

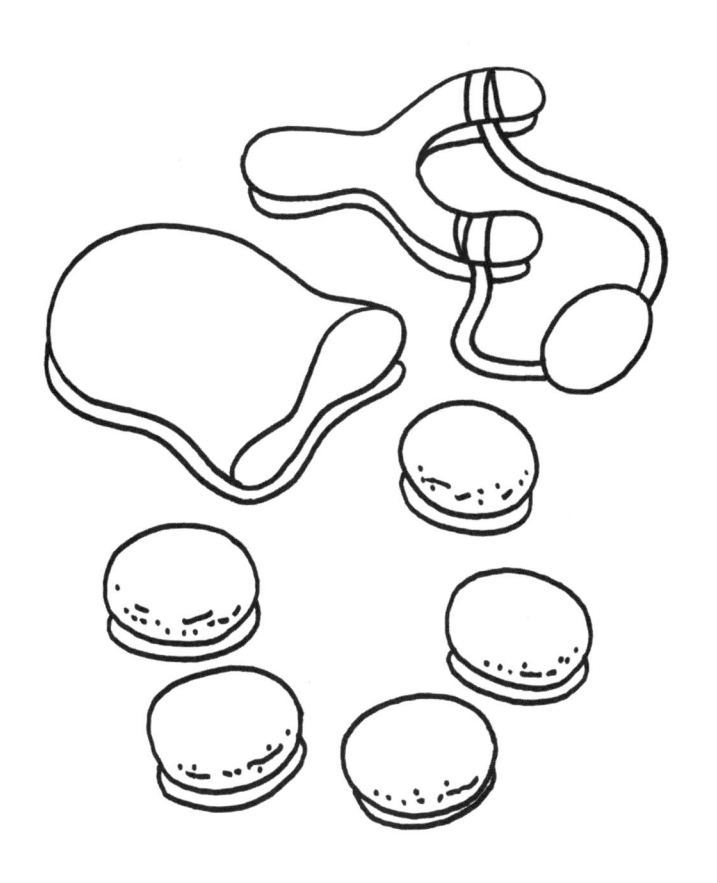

David took **5 (FIVE)** stones with him to fight the giant, Goliath.

1 Samuel 17

Jesus turned **6 (SIX)** jars of water into wine.

John 2:1-11

Pharaoh had a dream about **7 (SEVEN)** fat cows and thin cows.

Genesis 41:1-40

Josiah was only **8 (EIGHT)** years old when he became king.

2 Kings 22

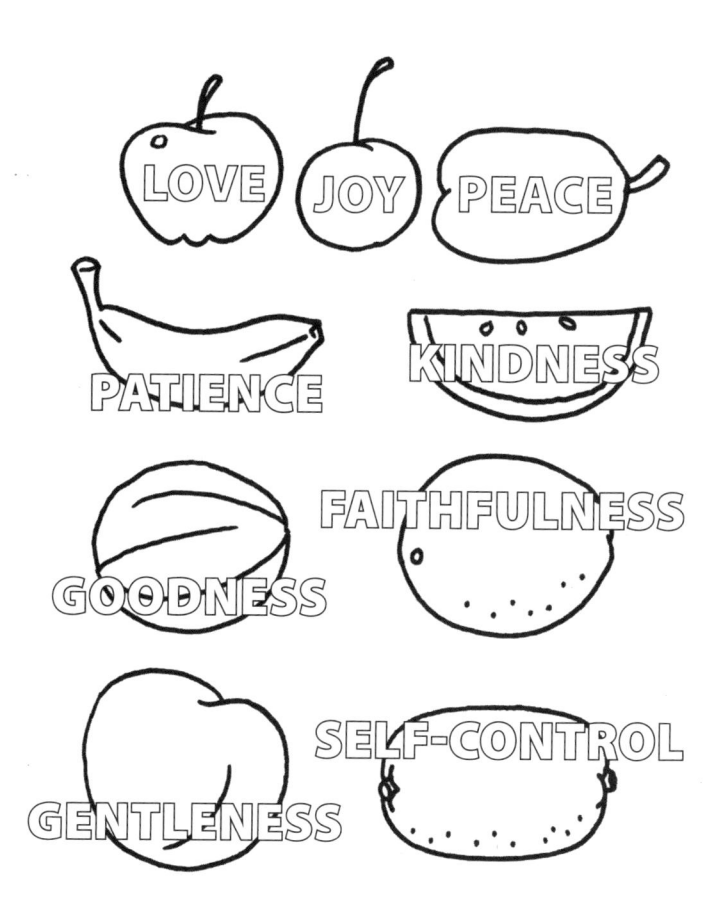

LOVE JOY PEACE
PATIENCE KINDNESS
GOODNESS FAITHFULNESS
GENTLENESS SELF-CONTROL

When we love Jesus, we will have **9 (NINE)** good things in our lives. We call these the Fruit of the Spirit.

Galatians 5:22-23

1. Do not worship any other gods besides me.
2. Do not make idols of any kind.
3. Do not misuse the name of the Lord your God.
4. Remember to keep the Sabbath day holy.
5. Honor your father and mother.
6. Do not murder.
7. Do not commit adultery.
8. Do not steal.
9. Do not lie about your neighbor.
10. Do not covet.

God gave us **10 (TEN)** commandments to help us live happy lives.

Exodus 20:1-17

Joseph dreamed that **11 (ELEVEN)** stars were bowing down to him.

Genesis 37:1-11

Jesus chose **12 (TWELVE)** disciples to help Him with His work.

It took Solomon **13 (THIRTEEN)** years to build his palace.

1 Kings 7:1-12

Paul was on a ship when a storm lasted for
14 (FOURTEEN) days. God promised everyone would be safe.

Acts 27

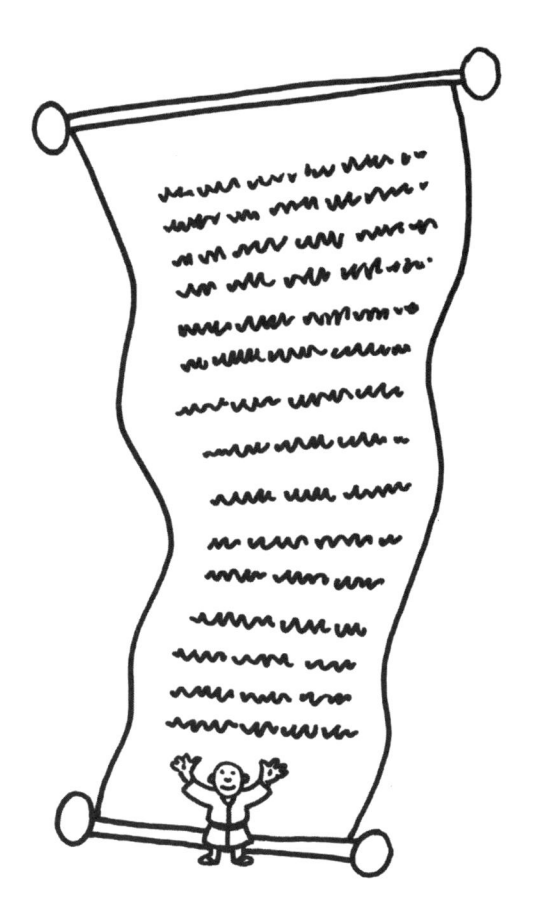

In a dream, Zechariah the prophet saw a flying scroll that was 30 feet long and **15 (FIFTEEN)** feet wide.

Zechariah 5:1-4

Colors of the Bible

God must really like bright colors because He made so many of them! Which color is your favorite? Let's see how many more colors we can learn.

Color this picture using your favorite color.

GREEN
God made the world and everything in it.

Genesis 1

Color the plants and trees GREEN.

RED

Esau begged his brother Jacob for a bowl of red stew.

Genesis 25:27-34

Color the bowl RED.

SILVER

Joseph told a servant to put his silver cup in his brother's sack.

Genesis 44

Color the cup SILVER.

ORANGE

Moses heard God speaking to him from a burning bush.

Exodus 3:1-6

Color the bush ORANGE.

GRAY

David took five stones and went to fight the giant, Goliath.

1 Samuel 17

Color the stones GRAY.

BLUE
The king had a party in the palace garden.

Esther 1:1-8

Color the curtains BLUE.

GOLD

King Nebuchadnezzar made a HUGE gold statue, but Shadrach, Meshach and Abednego would only worship God.

Daniel 3

Color the statue GOLD.

BLACK

Jonah was swallowed by a big fish because he wouldn't obey God.

Jonah 1

Color the big fish BLACK.

YELLOW

Wise men saw a bright star in the sky when Baby Jesus was born.

Matthew 2:1-12

Color the star YELLOW.

WHITE

An angel came and rolled the stone away from the empty tomb.
He told Jesus' friends, "Jesus has risen!"

Matthew 28:1-7

Color the angel WHITE.

BROWN

Jesus fed 5,000 men with five loaves of bread and two fish.

Luke 6:30-44

Color the loaves of bread BROWN.

PINK

The prodigal son spent all his money and had to get a job feeding pigs.

Luke 15:11-32

Color the pigs PINK.

PURPLE

Lydia sold purple cloth. One day she heard Paul preach, and she asked Jesus to live in her heart.

Acts 16:11-15

Color the cloth PURPLE.